Contents

The Blues

① The blues is a feeling

You can learn to play the blues in two ways. Formal music teaching will explore Western musical theory, and how the influence of African traditions created the idea of "blue" notes. You can learn to play minor pentatonic scales and how to work with the harmonic structures of tonic, dominant and subdominant chords.

This is not how Sonny Boy Williamson II or Little Walter learned to play, at least not directly.

Most of the great blues players learned to play by watching and listening to other great blues players. Technique came by trial and error, though some were fortunate to be shown how to play specific licks by their friends and mentors; hence the Sonny Boy Williamson influence you can hear in Howlin' Wolf's playing.

This aural tradition has a major advantage over the formal school. It helps winnow out those who do not have a feel for the blues, or who are not drawn to it by its emotional power. Why would you bother to play it, if it doesn't speak to your soul?

So in this book, the best I can do is give you some basic techniques for playing some of the things you've heard on recording or at gigs. It's up to you to take the raw material and use it to create your personal journey into the blues. As the man said, if it's in you, it's got to come out.

Blues power

Before we get down to some specific lessons, it is worth taking a brief look at the history and legacy of the blues. As a blues player, you will be part of a long line of musicians who have been playing the music for more than 100 years. And as I said at the beginning, it's not enough to play the notes; the blues is about feeling – the notes come later.

I still get asked how I, a white, middle-aged Englishman, can possibly have a feel for an essentially African music, born of slavery and exploitation.

My answer is that blues is about power. It's true that it was the African slaves in the Southern States of America who first began to play the music that became known as blues, but I don't believe it was a music of suffering or surrender. It became a powerful assertion of identity and strength, which is why it went all around the world and influenced everyone from Bob Dylan, Elvis Presley and the Beatles, to Miles Davis, George Gershwin and Jimi Hendrix.

My band, Storm Warning, tours the UK and Europe. Everywhere, we meet fans who love the blues, many of whom first heard it when pioneers like Paul Jones, John Mayall and Alexis Korner introduced it to the UK in the 1960s. It was as much the soundtrack to their own assertion of identity and independence as it had been for the slaves nearly a century earlier.

Where the blues began

Flourishing first as a popular folk music among the black population in the Southern States, the blues moved north during the depression of the early 1930s. The struggling farmers and plantation workers in the South rode the trains to Chicago in search of new employment and better living conditions.

In the city, the music became louder and tougher. The arrival of electric guitars and amplification gave traditional stylists like Muddy Waters and Little Walter new sounds to work with, and the Chicago sound, immortalized by the Chess label recordings of the 1940s and 1950s, was born. Rock and roll was not far behind…

The other source of power within the blues is the fact that it takes the universal issues of life as its subject matter, expressing them in a deceptively simple and direct way. If you've been in love, worked hard in a job, struggled to pay rent, gone on long journeys, raised children, driven a car, or done any of the ordinary and extraordinary things life brings, then the blues has something to say to you – if you want to hear it.

Starting Blues Harmonica

by Stuart "Son" Maxwell

AMSCO PUBLICATIONS
part of The Music Sales Group
London / New York / Paris / Sydney / Copenhagen / Berlin / Madrid / Tokyo

First note

To get the best out of this book and CD, you will need a diatonic harmonica tuned to the key of C. This is one of the most common blues keys, so you will get plenty of use from your harmonica. If you want to know what "diatonic" means, you will find out later in the book.

As this book is about the blues harmonica, I have used the blues term "harp" in some places. It is slang, but it's the blues.

You don't have to learn to read music to play the pieces, but if you want an idea of how to do it, there is a bit on music theory at the end of the book.

But now, grab your harp and get ready to blow some blues.

Published by
Amsco Publications
257 Park Avenue South, New York, NY 10010 USA

Exclusive Distributor in the United States, Canada, Mexico and U.S. possessions:
Hal Leonard Corporation
7777 West Bluemound Road, Milwaukee, WI 53213, USA.

Exclusive Distributors for the rest of the World:
Music Sales Limited
Distribution Centre, Newmarket Road, Bury St Edmunds,
Suffolk IP33 3YB, UK.
Music Sales Pty Limited
20 Resolution Drive, Caringbah, NSW 2229, Australia.

Order No. AM999350
ISBN 978-0-8256-3732-2
HL Item Number: 14031349

This book © Copyright 2009 Amsco Publications,
a division of Music Sales Corporation

Editor: Rachel Payne
Original design: Kathy Gammon
Cover design and layout: Fresh Lemon
Pictures courtesy of: Terry Cryer/Corbis, Karlheinz Kluter, LFI,
Diane Diederich/iStock and David Redfern/Redferns.

Printed in the United States of America by Vicks Litho

Your Guarantee of Quality
As publishers, we strive to produce every book to the highest commercial standards. The music has been freshly engraved and the book has been carefully designed to minimize awkward page turns and to make playing from it a real pleasure. Particular care has been given to specifying acid-free, neutral-sized paper made from pulps which have not been elemental chlorine bleached. This pulp is from farmed sustainable forests and was produced with special regard for the environment. Throughout, the printing and binding have been planned to ensure a sturdy, attractive publication which should give years of enjoyment. If your copy fails to meet our high standards, please inform us and we will gladly replace it.

www.musicsales.com

Feelin' round for the blues

 This section is for true beginners – if this is the first time you've tried playing the harmonica, it's a quick way to make a bluesy sound.

Pick up your harp and make sure you've got the low notes on the left-hand side. If your harp has numbers on it, the numbers should be on the top with hole number 1 on the left.

Put your mouth over holes 3, 4 and 5 and suck gently. You are playing a group of notes (called a *chord*), which for now we'll call G7. You can hear what it should sound like on Track 2.

It's the slightly jarring sound of the 4 and the 5 notes that is actually at the heart of the blues; the 5 hole makes a blue note.

Don't stop at G7; just try blowing and sucking up and down the harp, seeing how it feels and sounds. You'll find it is easier to play the lower notes. The higher notes are made with shorter reeds (more about reeds later) so they need a bit more breath. You'll probably also find that some notes choke if you play too hard. Get used to blowing and sucking until you are getting a fairly smooth and consistent sound.

Playing harmonica with your ears

Your ears are as vital as your mouth when you are playing the harmonica. First, you need to listen to every harp player you can find, so you can stretch your repertoire of licks, riffs and chops. It's not about copying, it's about learning the language of the blues harp and then making it your own.

Second, when you are playing with a band, you need to be aware of what's happening around you. Harp players are notorious for playing across everything no matter what. You can spot the good ones, because they know when to shut up. Leaving space in the music gives it greater power, and it also means you make a bigger impact when it is your turn to cut loose.

Lesson 1: Learning to play

 Now it's time to start the real work.

Holding the harmonica

First of all, check that you are holding the harmonica properly.

Hold your harmonica as shown in the picture.

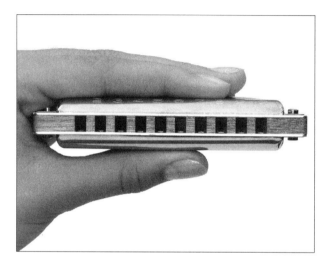

It doesn't really matter which hand you use, as long as you have a good grip on your harmonica and can put the other hand around the back to cup the sound, as shown here.

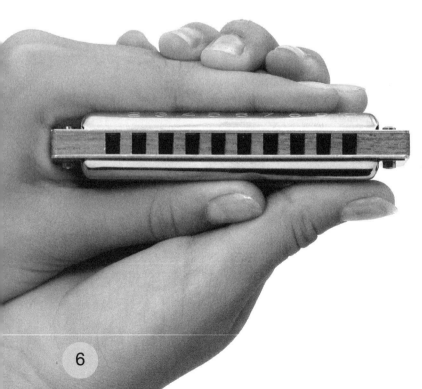

Make sure there is enough of the harmonica sticking out from between your fingers and thumb to allow you to get your lips well over the holes. Get comfortable, and you should have something like the harmonica grip shown here.

4) **Blowing and drawing**

Next, think about your breathing. You have to breathe deep, and not just suck and push the air through your lips. The proper word is *draw*, rather than suck, because you draw breath right down inside you; it should feel as though you are breathing with your abdomen as well as your mouth and lungs. If your cheeks and lips are doing all the work, you will quickly get tired and short of breath.

Got you tabbed

Now here's the first tune. It's a simple one, just to get you used to blowing and drawing, and moving round the harp. You will play two notes at a time; practise shaping your mouth to make sure others don't sneak in round the edges.

Notice also that some notes are played with a click of the tongue; I'm making a "duh" with the tip of my tongue as I blow and draw. This is one of several techniques you can use to emphasize a note or chord; we'll look at others later.

Also, this is your introduction to our version of harmonica tablature, or *tab* – the signs and symbols that show you how to play without having to read music.

The up arrows are blow notes: ▲
The down arrows are draw notes: ▼
The double arrows are bent notes
(more on these in a minute): ▼
The arrows with two heads are bends
down and back up again (more later on
these too): ▲▼

The lines underneath tell you if it is a long note (like this: –) or a shorter note (like this: -), but use your ears to hear exactly how it should sound.

The tab is divided into sections called *bars*. In music, bars help you to work out the rhythm; there is a set number of beats to count in each bar. For this book, you don't need to worry about this, since you are using your ears to get the rhythm, but the bars are useful anyway because they break the tab up and make it easier to read. You also have the key and the time signature: there's more on these at the end of the book.

So here we go; try Track 5–6,
The Two-Timing Blues.

 ## The Two-Timing Blues

Key: **G**
Time: **4/4**
Feel: **Gentle shuffle**

G				G				G				G			
3-4	3-4	4-5	4-5	3-4	3-4	4-5	4-5	3-4	3-4	4-5	4-5	3-4	3-4	4-5	4-5
▼	▼	▲	▼	▼	▼	▲	▼	▼	▼	▲	▼	▼	▼	▲	▼
–	-	–	–	–	-	–	–	–	-	–	–	–	-	–	–

C7				C7				G				G			
4-5	4-5	4-5	5-6	4-5	4-5	4-5	5-6	3-4	3-4	4-5	4-5	3-4	3-4	4-5	4-5
▲	▲	▼	▲	▲	▲	▼	▲	▼	▼	▲	▼	▼	▼	▲	▼
–	–	–	–	–	–	–	–	–	-	–	–	–	-	–	–

D				C7				G								G		
3-4	3-4	3-4	3-4	3-4	3-4	3-4	3-4	2-3	2-3	2-3	2-3	2-3	2-3	2-3	2-3	2-3	3-4	2-3
▼	▼	▼	▼	▲	▲	▲	▲	▼	▼	▼	▼	▼	▼	▼	▼	▼	▲	▼
–	-	–	-	–	-	–	-	-	-	-	-	-	-	-	-	–	-	–

⑦ Single notes

Playing one note instead of several notes together all depends on the shape and size of your mouth. You have to try by pursing your lips around the harmonica until you find a shape that is comfortable and allows you to make a clean and rich single note.

You will have to find the shape that is right for your mouth. If the hole in your lips is too small, you will choke the note. If it is too large, you will find other notes creeping in. So keep trying, changing the shape of your lips and where you hold the harmonica, until you are getting a clean single note like the one on Track 8 – the note C, played by blowing the fourth hole.

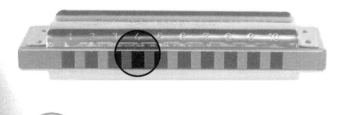

⑧

4
▲

⑨ Bending and wailing

If you listen to the great blues harp players, you will hear the harmonica wailing and crying as they play. These sounds are usually made by bending the reed inside the harmonica with your breath. It's not that difficult, but it's one of the hardest things you will have to learn, so let's get it out of the way now.

You have been blowing a single note on the fourth hole. To start wailing, try drawing a single note on the fourth hole. It's the note D.

To bend the note, you have to change the shape of your mouth and tongue, so that the air comes through the harp in a different way. Once again, it will depend on the size and shape of your mouth, so you will have to try a few times before it works.

Try curling the back of your tongue up toward the back of your mouth; your lower jaw might move forward a bit at the same time, which is fine. You will probably need to draw a little harder too, remembering to breathe deep. Keep changing the shape of your mouth until you find the note beginning to drop.

Once you've got it, you will quickly find that you can bend the note quite easily. Try gently bending and unbending the note; it should sound like Track 9.

One-Note Wail

So now here's the second tune to play. Listen to it, then try playing along with it.

 ## The One-Note Wail

Key: **G**
Time: **4/4**
Feel: **Medium country style**

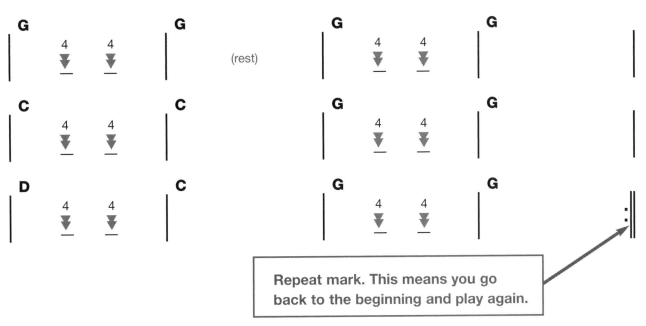

Repeat mark. This means you go back to the beginning and play again.

Lesson 2: Cross harp

(12) We have to touch on some basic music theory here, but it does help to understand the main secret of blues harp playing. The secret is that you mainly use draw notes, rather than blow notes, to play the blues.

Music is arranged in keys, which are given the same letters as the notes: A, B, C, D, E, F, G. The key tells you which notes fit best with the song. The notes in the key make a scale, the immortal do, re, mi, fa, so, la, ti, do. This is called the *diatonic* scale, which is where your harmonica gets its name from. On your C harp, the first blow note is C, the root of the C major scale.

When you play the scale of C major and the chord of C major (a group of notes, C, E and G) at the same time, it sounds relentlessly cheerful. Great for folk or country music, no good for blues, as Track 13 demonstrates:

(13) ## C chord and scale

(14) To unleash the emotional power of the blues, we play what's known by theorists as a *minor pentatonic* scale over the cheery major chord.

The trouble is, you can't play this scale easily by blowing a diatonic harmonica (known as playing the harp in *first position*). But if you try drawing and blowing on your C harp, rather than blowing and drawing, you can actually play in the key of G and get the blue notes you need. The draw on the second hole then becomes the root.

So when the rest of the band is playing in G, you need a C harp. That's why it is called *cross harp* (or *second position*). You are playing it backwards, or crosswise, or whatever you want to call it, but you are playing the blues.

The cross-harp principle applies to all keys. Here's a quick guide to show which harp goes with which key, when playing is crossed:

Second position

Key	A	B	C	D	E	F	G
Harp	D	E	F	G	A	B♭	C

The number of the blues

Your diatonic harp is actually even more adaptable. You can play it in a third and even a fourth position. These positions are particularly good when accompanying songs in minor keys.

Third position

We're getting dangerously into theory here, but you really don't need to know the technicalities unless you're interested. The plain facts are that in third position, you're using the draw on the first hole as the root. On a C harp, it's D, and you're roughly playing in the key of D minor. When accompanying a song in D or D minor, you can get some great plaintive wails. Here's a chart showing which harps go with which keys in third position:

Third position – major or minor keys

Key	A	B	C	D	E	F	G
Harp	G	A	B♭	C	D	E♭	F

Fourth position

Here, the blow note on hole 2 is the root. On your C harp, it's E and you can accompany songs in E or E minor:

Fourth position – major or minor keys

Key	A	B	C	D	E	F	G
Harp	F	G	A♭	B♭	C	D♭	E♭

You'll need to experiment with these positions to find out which holes work and which don't, depending on whether you are accompanying a song in a minor or major key. We're not going to use these positions in this book anyway, but the charts will come in handy later as you start to explore the blues harp in your own way.

The I, the IV and the V

We need to cover one final piece of blues theory before we move on, and it concerns song structure. The basic blues song is built around a sequence of 12 bars of music, with four beats to each bar. Countless rock and roll songs follow the same sequence and you probably recognize it anyway. This may be one of the other secrets of blues power; the 12-bar sequence seems to speak to something essential in us.

Bluesmen talk about the "one," the "four" and the "five" (written as I, IV and V). It's a shorthand for the three chords that make up the classic 12-bar song. *The Crying Blues* (p12) uses this typical sequence. The I is the root (G in *The Crying Blues*) and the IV is the second chord in the sequence (C). It's called IV because it's four steps up from the root on a diatonic scale. V is the third of the three chords – five steps up, giving us D in the *The Crying Blues*.

By referring to the I, the IV and the V, you can fit in quickly with almost any blues song in any key, even if it doesn't follow a conventional 12-bar sequence. You can sometimes hear musicians helping out new members of the band, or guests, by calling out "back to the five" or whatever the chord might be, so they know where to go even if they've never played the song before.

So here's a chart showing which chords are which in the most common blues keys:

	I	IV	V
A	A	D	E
B	B	E	F♯
C	C	F	G
D	D	G	A
E	E	A	B
F	F	B♭	C
G	G	C	D

It's useful to know where to find the root notes of these chords as a starting point for any accompaniment or soloing you might find yourself doing. Here's the chart for second position on any standard diatonic harp, in any key:

I   Draw hole 2 (or blow 3, when you need it)
IV Blow hole 1 or hole 4
V   Draw hole 1 or hole 4

We could stop now. Armed with this basic knowledge, you simply have to experiment and play along with recordings, or any amenable musicians you can find, and see for yourself what these simple principles have made possible. However, there are some more shortcuts and tricks of the trade we can work with to add some color and dimension to your style.

Lesson 3: Wah it's all about

 **15** Paul Jones, one of the first British bluesmen and a highly influential harp player, once likened the harmonica to "the sound of a human being in a high state of emotion." The wah-wah effect is one of the most powerful elements of the uniquely expressive language he was referring to.

Back in the days when the blues began, the slaves worked on cotton plantations. Blowing across the flatlands of the Mississippi delta, they would hear the whistles of trains, the cries and shouts of children, the howling of dogs and the calls of other creatures. The sounds of the trains were especially poignant – they spoke of prosperity and a better life up north in Chicago.

One of the legacies of the African tradition in the blues is the use of instruments to imitate the sounds of the world around. The harp is great for this, because bending the notes, changing the shape of the mouth and moving the cupping hand give it a remarkable vocal quality.

Noah Lewis's "Chickasaw Special" or Junior Wells's live version of "Little Red Rooster" are fine examples of this, and we will experiment with creating similar sounds now.

Start with a draw on hole 4, opening and closing your cupping hand. The more airtight the chamber when your hand is closed, the better the effect will be.

One of the things that makes the harmonica unique is the fact that the mouth and hands contribute most to the sound. They form a chamber that acts as the sound box of your harp; any little variations you make in the shape of the chamber will alter the sound, subtly or dramatically.

Try bending the note up and down as you move your hand, and alter the speed of your hand. You should find the note really starts to wail and cry. Practice a few times, try some other holes and some chords, and then try the tunes on Tracks 16 and 18.

16–17 The Crying Blues

Key: **G**
Time: **4/4**
Feel: **Slow blues**

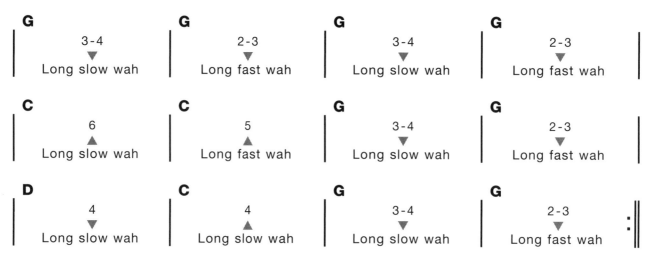

18-19 The Fox Chase Blues

Key: **G**
Time: **4/4**
Feel: **Bouncy country style**

This means you go back to the beginning and stop when you come to *Fine*.

Lesson 4: Riffing the blues

 The word "riff" is probably a derivative of "refrain," which in music theory means a repeated verse or a pattern of notes. There are some riffs that you just have to know if you are going to play the blues harp. They appear in countless songs, changed a bit here and there, but sounding very like each other.

The tunes here contain versions of two of the most important riffs; we've created our own interpretations, but they give you the essential sound.

It's well worth finding the originals of the songs on which these riffs are based – they are still widely available – and working out the riffs as played by Little Walter, Walter Horton and others.

Track 21 is *The Hoodoo Blues*, which has a "stopping" riff in it. The idea has been used on songs like "Walking By Myself," "Hoochie Coochie Man" and even rock and roll songs like "Blue Suede Shoes."

The Hoodoo Blues

Key: **G**
Time: **12/8**
Feel: **Heavy shuffle**

Track 24 draws on traditional Delta blues themes that were adapted for songs like "Rollin' And Tumbling" and "Louisiana Blues."

 Tumblin' Blues

Key: **G**
Time: **4/4**
Feel: **Quick shuffle**

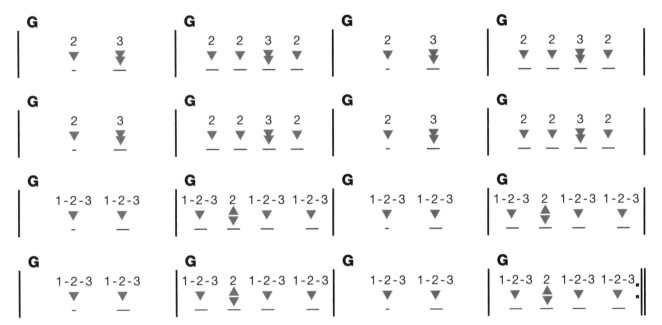

CHECKPOINT
WHAT YOU'VE ACHIEVED SO FAR

You can now:
- Read harmonica tab
- Bend single notes
- Play "cross harp"
- Play tunes using the "wah" effect
- Play standard blues riffs

Lesson 5: Chords and effects

26 If you play more than one note at a time, you're playing a chord. We've already used chords in some of the earlier pieces, but we're going to look at them in a bit more detail now, because they are useful ways of adding dynamics and style to your playing. They are also essential for accompaniment.

I'm not going to waste your time or mine working out the proper names for all the chords you can play, though on your C harp you've really only got chords based on C and G to choose from. What we're going to do here is practice playing chords as accompaniment and as ways of making solos more interesting.

Chords also help with sound effects. *The Fox Chase Blues* featured chords, and in the pieces that follow we'll make train noises and chicken noises.

We'll start on Track 27 with chickens or, more correctly, roosters. We're back to blues power here. Roosters strut around the chicken run as though they own the place – and they have the pick of the chickens. Again drawing on African tradition, early blues players adopted roosters as potent symbols of their own animal power.

So here's another version of a classic blues riff, featuring rooster and chicken sounds. For the rooster, use a bit of wah-wah with your hand and try pursing your lips to change the way the note sounds. You can bend the note a bit too. For the chicken sounds, try going "duck-duck-duck" as you draw. This is the only book that will show you how to make a chicken with a duck.

Rooster Blues

Key: **G**
Time: **12/8**
Feel: **Heavy, slow shuffle**

G					G					G					G			
4	4-5	4-5			4	4-5	4-5			4	4-5	4-5			4	4-5	4-5		
▼	▼	▼			▼	▼	▼			▼	▼	▼			▼	▼	▼		
-	—	—			-	—	—			-	—	—			-	—	—		

C / C / G / G
3 4 3 3 3 3 | 3 4 3 3 3 3 | 4 4-5 4-5 | 4 4-5 4-5 3 4

D / C / G / D
4 4-5 4 3 2 | 3 3 3 3 3 3 3 3 | 2 2 2 2 2 2 2 2 2 2 | 2 4 4

G / G / G / G
4 4-5 4-5 | 4 4-5 4-5 | 4 4-5 4-5 | 4 4-5 4-5

C / C / G / G
3 4 3 3 3 3 | 3 4 3 3 3 3 | 4 4-5 4-5 | 4 4-5 4-5 3 4

D / C / G / G
4 4-5 4 3 2 | 3 3 3 3 3 3 3 3 | 2 2 2 2 2 2 2 2 2 2 | 2 2-3 2-3

29 Track 30 brings us to the *train*. If you can't make like a train with a blues harp, you might as well give up now.

30–31 **Train Gone Blues**

Key: **G**
Time: **4/4**
Feel: **Bright country bounce**

We use chords to make the sound of the engine and clattering track. We've also got our duck back, this time making the chug-chug sound, though you could try saying "chug-chug" as well. Chords and bends are also needed to make the sad sound of the whistle echoing across the plantation, or back down the track to the guy desolate on the platform, deep in the blues. You'll need to bend the notes too, to get that real crying sound.

Introduction *Repeat introduction four times*

G	G	G	G
2 1-2-3 1-2-3 1-2-3	1-2-3 1-2-3 1-2-3 1-2-3	2 1-2-3 1-2-3 1-2-3	1-2-3 1-2-3 1-2-3 1-2-3

Main Theme

G	G	G	G
3-4 3-4	4 3	3-4	

G	G	G	G
3-4 3-4	4 3	3-4	

C	C	C	C
4-5 4-5	5 4	4-5 4-5	5 4

G	G	G	G
3-4 3-4	4 3	3-4	

D	D	C	C
4-5 4-5	4	4 4	3

To Repeat *Repeat main theme*

G	G	G	G
2 1-2-3 1-2-3 1-2-3	2 1-2-3 1-2-3 1-2-3	2 1-2-3 1-2-3	

To Finish

G	G	G	G
2 1-2-3 1-2-3 1-2-3	2 1-2-3 1-2-3 1-2-3	2 1-2-3 1-2-3	2 2-3-4 1-2-3

Track 33 is the *Chicago Blues*. Chicago was the promised land for Southern blues players, with the chance of better employment and living conditions. But the clubs and bars in the urban environment were louder than the rural juke joints, so it was here that players like Muddy Waters and Little Walter Jacobs first began to use electric guitars, microphones and amplifiers.

You are not playing the tune here – it's the piano that has the lead – but you are playing along with chords that fit the music.

The classic Chicago style draws on the same traditions as early jazz – which was developing in Chicago at the same time – in that the musicians improvised independently around the central theme of the song, while creating a cohesive, compelling sound. It's about playing with your ears; the great Chicago groups like The Aces, Muddy Waters's band, and modern bands like Nick Moss and the Flip Tops, play all together, yet without ever intruding into one another's space.

There's also a new effect here: the *trill*. This is another basic harp effect that features in countless urban and rural blues performances. Move the harp quickly from side to side in your mouth, so that two holes next to each other make the trill. You'll need to practice getting a good clean trilling sound; make sure each note sounds clearly and try not to let other notes sneak in. It's marked in the tab with the arrows between the holes, like this: 4<>5. Some harp players suggest playing trills by moving your head from side to side, but frankly it gives me a headache and a pain in the neck. Let the harp do the work.

 Chicago Blues

Key: **G**
Time: **12/8**
Feel: **Heavy shuffle**

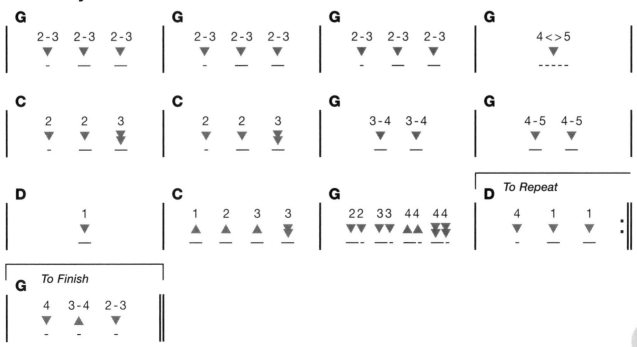

Lesson 6: Good vibes

(35) There are two main types of wobbles in the basic blues harp arsenal. *Vibrato* is where the actual pitch of the note moves up and down. *Tremolo* is where you use your breath to break up the note in rapid bursts. Track 37, **The Moody Blues**, gives you the chance to use both wobbles.

The key point to make about vibrato in particular is not to over use it. If every note is wobbling, it quickly becomes irritating to listen to, and the effect is wasted. But a well-timed and paced vibrato dropped in at the end of a long note is a spine-tingling source of blues power.

Vibrato is a form of bend, but it involves the tip of the tongue rather than the back. Essentially, you need to say "yuh-yuh-yuh" as you draw or blow a note. As always, experiment with your tongue and jaw to find a way that works for you.

(36) Tremolo is a real test of your breathing technique, because it has to come from right down in your abdomen. Draw your breath in little jerks; try going "uh-uh-uh" right at the back of your throat, and further down, if you can. You should feel it in your stomach muscles to get the real depth of emotional impact.

Track 37, **The Moody Blues**, is based on "Mighty Long Time," by the greatest blues harmonica player of all, Sonny Boy Williamson II. You'll find it on his album *King Biscuit Time*, and it's one of the finest expressions of blues power ever recorded.

Key: **G**
Time: **4/4**
Feel: **Slow, dark blues**

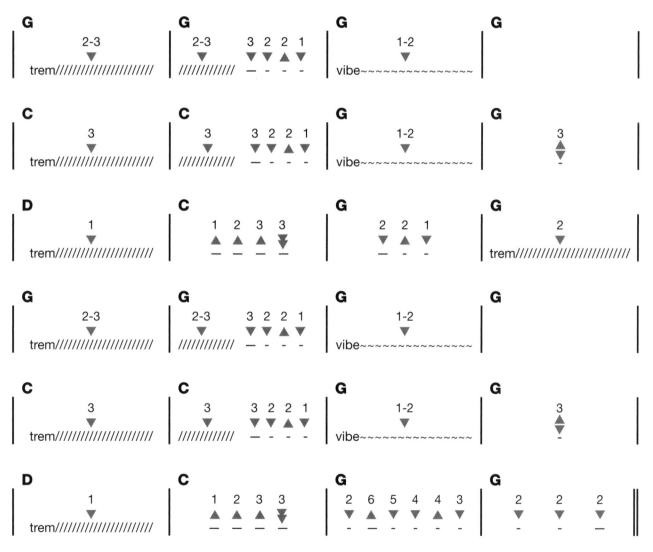

Lesson 7: Blow away your blues

39 Finally, some jam tracks to play along with. This is where Storm Warning finally gets a chance to cut loose, but we've managed to shut them up enough to give you room to stretch out. These are exercises in improvisation, with plenty of space to play around with the basic techniques you've learned so far.

Improvising means using your ears more than ever. You have to listen to the music and make sure your playing is sympathetic with the mood and tone, and you have to know when to keep quiet.

The magic of improvisation is that the further you get from the tune, the more chance there is of something special happening in the music. This is the essence of blues power; when you are part of a group of musicians improvising

together, it can be like riding a huge internal rollercoaster, with unimaginable highs of creativity.

The only way to learn the craft of improvisation is to practice, practice, practice. With these jam tracks, you can start off copying what I'm playing and then gradually add your own ideas. The more you add, the less room there will be for the original parts, until everything you are playing is coming from you.

Notice also that there are solos for the guitar and the keyboards. These are opportunities for you to practice the gentle art of not playing at all, or to work out some unobtrusive accompaniments.

So here we are – four classic blues styles for you to play with until you are out of breath.

 **City Blues Jam**

Key: **G**
Time: **12/8**
Feel: **Quick shuffle**

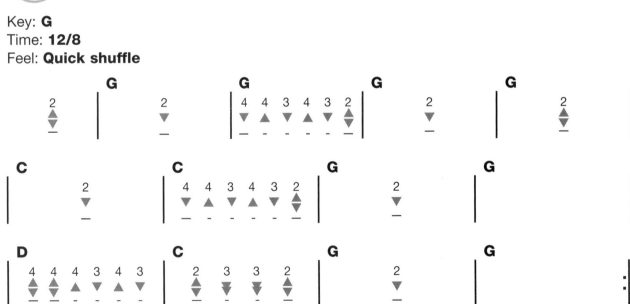

 **Midnight Blues Jam**

Key: **G**
Time: **4/4**
Feel: **Slow, dark blues**

Dm6	Gm6	Dm6	Dm6
4 5 4 3	6 5 5 5	4	

Gm6	Gm6	Dm6	Dm6
6 5 5 3 2	6 5 5 4 2	3	4 5 4

Am6	Gm6	Dm6 Gm6	Am6
5 5 4 5 4	6 5 5 4 5 3	2 3 4 4 5 6	6 5 4

 **Swinging Blues Jam**

Key: **G**
Time: **4/4**
Feel: **Swinging blues**

	G	G	G	G
4 5 4 5	6 6 4 5 4 5	6 6 4 5 4 5	6 6 5 5 4 5 3 2	4 5 4 5

C	C	G	G
6 6 4 5 4 5	6 6 4 5 4 5	6 6 5 5 4 5 3 2	4 5 4

D	C	G	G
5 5 5 4 5 4	6 5 5 4 5 3 2	2 2 2 2 2 2	2 1 1

 **Rocking Blues Jam**

Key: **G**
Time: **12/8**
Feel: **Rocking blues**

G	G	G	G
6 6 6 6 6 6 6 6 6 6 6 6	3 2	6 6 6 6 6 6 6 6 6 6 6 6	3 3 3 2

C	C	G	G
4 4 3 3 3 4 4 4 3 3 3	4 4 3 3 3 4 4 4 3 3 3	6 6 6 6 6 6 6 6 6 6 6 6	3 2 2 3 4

D	C	G	G
4 4 1 1	4 4 4 4 4 4 4 4 4 3	2 2 2 2 2 2 2 2 2 2	2 1 1

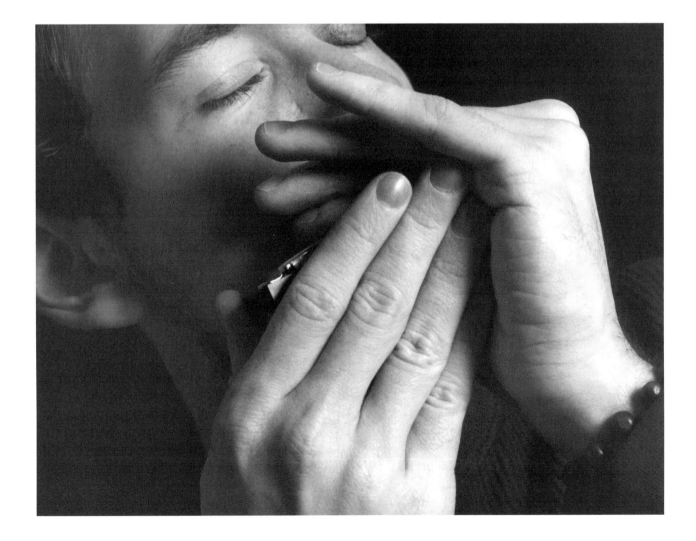

About harps

To get the best out of your harp, it's good to know how it works. Here's a quick guide, with some tips on care for your harp.

The harmonica is a "free reed" instrument. The sound comes from little strips of metal, or reeds, attached to a metal plate which is fixed onto the body of the harp over the holes. There are two reeds for each of the ten holes in a diatonic harp – ten on the top, ten on the bottom. It's called a free reed instrument because the sound is made by the reeds vibrating in the air. In ordinary reed instruments, like saxophones or clarinets, the sound is made by the reed vibrating against something. When you blow, the top reeds open and the bottom reeds close into their holes. When you draw, the bottom reeds open and the top reeds close up. It's as simple as that.

Playing a harmonica can be messy, so you should always tap the stuff out of your harmonica before you put it away. Also, it makes sense not to eat anything just before you are going to play, and drink only water while you are playing; sticky drinks, nuts and other things are not good for your harp.

If you find that some notes are not working properly you can, with care, gently lift the top and bottom covers off the harmonica to see the reed plates. Carefully check that the reeds are sitting neatly in their slots and that they are clean, with nothing to stop them from opening and shutting properly. You can clean them with a damp cotton swab, but take care not to leave any bits of cotton behind.

Which harp?

The Hohner Marine Band is generally reckoned to be the most popular diatonic harmonica. Certainly, it was the one coveted by most of the blues masters, though for people like Sonny Boy Williamson II, even a toy harp could be made to sound great. The key to buying harps is to find the one that suits you best, and you have to do it by trial and error. Some Hohner harps and the Lee Oskar series allow you to replace reed plates, which saves having to buy a whole new harp every time one finally bends its last note. Personally, I like Marine Bands best, just because they have the history, but I actually play Hohner Cross Harps on stage. They sound almost as good, and they have those replaceable plates…

Amplified harp

I spent hundreds of dollars trying to find the ideal combination of microphone and amplifier. The problem is getting enough volume to be heard above those wretched guitarists and drummers, while avoiding the curse of howling feedback.

Those who want the massive Walter Horton tone go for big amps with four 12-inch speakers in them, such as the Fender Bassman. They also use the classic bullet-style microphones, as made by Shure and Hohner. For me, however, the key message is this: whatever rig you use, your acoustic tone is the only thing that counts. Getting your sound right without an amplifier means that your amplified sound will be good too.

After trying several amps and microphones, I gave up and I now play through a good vocal microphone (a Beyer M69) and whatever PA is available. I also cheated and bought a cheap overdrive pedal for those numbers when I do want a more distorted sound. On several numbers, I sing and play through the same microphone. After all, the Chicago sound came about not because the harp players were looking for it, but because that's what the early equipment happened to sound like. They took it and developed it, but they started out with superb acoustic tones of their own.

When using a microphone, don't jam the harp against it; let it rest in the cup of your hand so there is an acoustic chamber between the harp and the microphone. It'll give you a better sound. An echo or reverb pedal is also useful, if none is available through the PA.

The great blues harp players

To play harmonica with your ears, you have to have something to listen to, so here are a few people who have made the blues harp one of the great sounds of modern music. Listen to these players, learn to play their riffs, and then mix them in to your own style. It's all part of learning the language of the blues, so that when you get up on stage with a blues band and they say "Louisiana Blues, in A," you'll know what to do…

Sonny Boy Williamson I

John Lee Williamson was the first harp player to achieve lasting national fame in America. He was recording from the 1930s until 1948, when he was murdered on his way home from a gig. His style was very popular and most of the harp players that came after him sounded a bit like him. Two of the best examples of his work can be found on "Good Morning Little Schoolgirl" and "Bluebird Blues."

Sonny Boy Williamson II

People argue over whether Rice Miller stole John Lee's "Sonny Boy" name, or John Lee stole his; certainly John Lee was the first famous Sonny Boy. But this Sonny Boy is a true master and, for many harp players (including me), the greatest of all. Notice how he plays only a few notes; it's all in the timing and the way he plays them. Nearly all Sonny Boy tracks are important but you must listen to "Mighty Long Time," "Help Me" and "Bring It On Home."

Sonny Terry

You don't have to be called Sonny to play blues harp, but it seems to help. Sonny Terry was the greatest harp player in the country style and his influence is still felt whenever people pick up a harp. He was blind and worked with other famous bluesmen like Brownie McGhee and Blind Boy Fuller, and he was a master of special effects, as well as a wonderful soloist and accompanist. Listen to his "Fox Chase" solo and his version of "Key To The Highway" with Brownie McGhee.

Little Walter

This magnificent player made the amplified harmonica sound famous, using special effects like echo and distortion to change the sound of his harp. He is the Jimi Hendrix of harp, because he redefined the sonic possibilities of the harmonica and pushed it to the frontline as an instrument. Essential tracks include "Juke," "Blue Light," and "Louisiana Blues," where he accompanies the great blues singer Muddy Waters.

Big Walter "Shakey" Horton

You could also change your name to "Walter," I suppose. Big Walter's tone is still widely imitated and his technique is staggeringly good. Like most of the top Chicago stylists, he worked with Muddy Waters, but he played some of his best solos as part of Jimmy Rogers' band. Look out for the solo cuts "Easy" and "Walter's Boogie."

Junior Wells

A protégé of Sonny Boy Williamson II, Junior Wells brought Chicago-style harp into the funkier era of the 1960s and 1970s. His sparse, punchy style made every note count, while his taught vocal style oozed power. "Hoodoo Man Blues" and "Hey Lawdy Mama" are among many essential cuts.

Other great players

There are too many to include all of them, of course, but look out for James Cotton, Noah Lewis and George "Harmonica" Smith, as well as white bluesmen like Paul Butterfield, Paul Jones, Rod Piazza, Kim Wilson, Charlie Musselwhite and Ron "Pigpen" McKernan of the Grateful Dead. You should also listen to Tony "Little Sun" Glover, who worked with "Spider" John Koerner and Dave "Snaker" Ray in Koerner, Ray and Glover. He wrote the best book of all on how to play blues harp, but it is no longer published, which is why you are stuck with me.

Basic music theory

Harmonica players who know which notes they are playing are quite rare and as a blues player you probably won't need to know much. But it is very useful to understand the basics of music theory, just so you can at least know what the guitarists and piano players are talking about. So here's a very quick introduction to the basics of reading music.

Beats and notes

This is a staff, which is made up of five lines called staff lines. The position of the note on the staff tells you how high or low the note is.

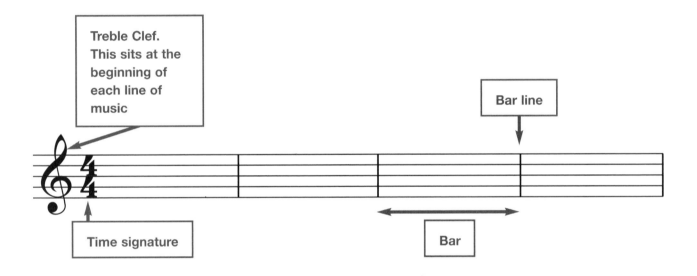

Treble Clef. This sits at the beginning of each line of music

Bar line

Time signature

Bar

C D E F G A B C

The dots and lines of the notes represent beats and indicate how long you should play each note for. Here are the most common dots you will see:

Quarter Note
One quarter note equals one beat.

Whole Note
Equals four quarter notes – hold the note for four beats.

Half Note
Equals two quarter notes – hold the note for two beats.

Eighth Note
Equals half a quarter note – hold the note for half a beat.

Sixteenth Note
Equals a quarter of a quarter note – hold the note for a quarter of a beat.

Time signature
The staff in the example on page 28 is divided into sections called *bars*. These are separated by *barlines*. Bars are needed to help show the rhythm of the music. Rhythm is measured by the number of beats in a bar. The rhythm used for a piece of music is known as its *time signature*.

The time signature of each piece of music tells you how to count the number of beats. The most widely-used time signature is 4/4, which means that there are four beats in the bar, each worth a quarter of a whole note. The first or top figure gives you the number of beats, and the bottom or lower figure tells you what each beat is worth – a half note, quarter note, eighth note and so on.

In this book, we have used 4/4 and 12/8. A time signature of 12/8 means there are 12 half-beats in the bar. You count 12/8 in little groups of threes (1-2-3, 1-2-3, 1-2-3, 1-2-3) to get the kind of shuffle rhythm used in hundreds of blues songs. You could also count it as a kind of swinging 4/4 with each of the 1s in the little groups being one beat of the four beats in the bar, but when you come to write the music down it is harder to make it work.

That's about as much as you need to know about music theory for now; there is a bit more on the subject in my other book, *The Complete Harmonica Player*, which is also published by Amsco Publications (AM977438). It includes a CD that features examples of different time signatures.

Nothing but the blues

 48 The blues has always been a music passed down from player to player, rather than written down by composers. You can write out blues songs, but you cannot capture what they are about unless you hear them. For example, playing Son House's song "Death Letter" by reading the music will never help you to understand the power of hearing him perform it.

This book is really only a starter, to help you understand how the harmonica works and give you some idea of how to play what you hear. But like the Sonnys and Walters that made the harp great, you are really on your own. You have to find your own way of playing, by listening and learning from records and hearing people like Paul Jones, Rod Piazza or Carey Bell performing live.

So keep your ears open, take a harp with you wherever you go, and enjoy discovering the power of the blues. Because the blues will get you someday, and you better be good and ready.

49 ## You have been warned

On the CD I am joined by the other members of the band that I play with, Storm Warning. They are Bob "Mad Dog" Moore on guitar, Derek White on the bass, Ian Salisbury on the keyboards and Roger Willis on the drums.

The band formed in 2004 and you can find out more about us at www.stormwarning.co.uk and hear our song "Bullets" on track 49.

Further playing

The Complete Harmonica Player
This great introduction to the harmonica focuses on the three most popular styles: blues, folk and country. Choose your favorite style to sound like Sonny Boy Williamson, John Mayall or Bob Dylan! Includes CD. Written by Stuart "Son" Maxwell
Order No. AM977438

Blues Harp From Scratch – Blues Harmonica for Absolute Beginners
This user-friendly CD-guidebook by Mick Kinsella includes all your favorite tunes such as "Amazing Grace" and "Oh Susanna," plus guidance on note-bending, blues riffs, wah-wah, note splitting, as well as loads of blues solos!
Order No. AM92630

Bob Dylan Harmonica
Thirty great songs – 24 for both diatonic and chromatic harmonica players, six for chromatic only. Includes: "Blowin' In The Wind," "Just Like A Woman" and "Under Your Spell."
Order No. AM932140

Instant Harmonica
Play the harmonica now, with the revolutionary *Instant Harmonica*. This book and accompanying audio will teach the beginner basic technique, popular tunes and blues playing, a little theory and some special effects used by professional players. No previous knowledge of music necessary.
Order No. AM967395

The Beatles Harmonica Songbook
Twenty-one of the Beatles's best songs arranged for chromatic harmonica. Complete lyrics to all the songs. Includes: "Eleanor Rigby," "Get Back," "Hey Jude" and "Let It Be."
Order No. NO90549

Pop Songs For Harmonica
Nineteen classic pop favorites newly arranged for harmonica solo. Includes "Blowin' In The Wind," "Bye Bye Love" and "Hey Jude." Ideal for beginners and players returning to the mouth organ. A great selection of classic pop songs for all music lovers! Contains complete lyrics and guitar chord boxes. Also includes simple hints and tips on how to hold the harmonica, breath control, notes on the harmonica, and the C scale.
Order No. AM87044

How To Play The Pocket Harmonica
Teaches from the very beginning to advanced techniques. Includes care of the harmonica and sections on riffs and soloing. Illustrated.
Order No. AM34521

Beginning Blues Harp With Don Baker
Renowned blues harmonica hero Don Baker teaches you how to play this versatile instrument from scratch. You will discover how to bend notes and achieve triplet-tonguing and expressive tone control. Also features a booklet of easy-to-follow notated examples.
Order No. DV10241

About the CD and track listing

The CD included contains spoken instructions and demonstrations to help you learn; it's like having your very own teacher! It demonstrates what the various techniques are supposed to sound like so you can listen carefully and match them up with your own playing. The CD also contains full demonstrations of all pieces with a real live band, plus backing tracks without the harmonica, so you can jam along with the band on your own. The first time you hear the piece, it will be the full demonstration, the second time will be the backing track only.

Have fun!

Track
1   The Blues
2   Feelin' round for the blues

Lesson 1 – Learning to play
3   Holding the harmonica
4   Blowing and drawing
5-6   The Two-Timing Blues
7   Single notes
8   Single note C
9   Bending and wailing
10-11 The One-Note Wail

Lesson 2 – Cross harp
12   Introduction to Cross Harp
13   C chord and scale
14   Cross Harp explained

Lesson 3 – Wah it's all about
15   Wah wah
16-17 The Crying Blues
18-19 The Fox Chase Blues

Lesson 4 – Riffing the blues
20   Riffing the blues
21-22 The Hoodoo Blues
23   Introduction to Tumblin' Blues
24-25 Tumblin' Blues

Lesson 5 – Chords and effects
26   The rooster
27-28 Rooster Blues
29   The train
30-31 Train Gone Blues
32   The trill
33-34 Chicago Blues

Lesson 6 – Good vibes
35   Vibrato
36   Tremolo
37-38 The Moody Blues

Lesson 7 – Blow away your blues
39   Improvisation
40-41 City Jam Blues
42-43 Midnight Blues Jam
44-45 Swinging Blues Jam
46-47 Rocking Blues Jam
48   Last Word
49   Storm Warning play "Bullets"